DESTINED TO BE:WALKING INTO YOUR GOD GIVEN DESTINY ONE STEP AT A TIME STUDY GUIDE

DANYELLE SCROGGINS

Unless otherwise indicated, Scriptures verses are from the taken King James Version of the Bible.

"Scripture quotations are taken from the New American Standard Bible®, Copyright © 1960, 1962, 1963, 1968, 1971, 1972, 1973, 1975, 1977, 1995 by The Lockman Foundation

Used by permission." (www.Lockman.org)

Published by:

Divinely Sown Publishing

DESTINED TO BE: Walking Into Your God Given Destiny One Step At A Time Study Guide

Copyright © 2024 Unless otherwise indicated, Scriptures verses are from the taken King James Version of the Bible.

All Rights Reserved. Printed in the United States of America. No part of this book may be used or reproduced in any manner whatsoever without written permission except in the case of brief quotations embodied in critical articles and reviews.

Special discounts are available for quantity purchases. For details contact the publisher at the address above.

Published by: Divinely Sown Publishing

DESTINED TO BE:WALKING INTO YOUR GOD GIVEN DESTINY ONE STEP AT A TIME STUDY GUIDE

Copyright © 2024 by Danyelle Scroggins

First Edition paperback

10 9 8 7 6 5 4 3 2 1

Printed in the United States of America

Book Cover Design by Danyelle Scroggins

Exclusive discounts are available for quantity purchases. For details, contact the publisher at the address above.

Printed in the United States of America

ABOUT DESTINED TO BE: WALKING INTO YOUR GOD GIVEN DESTINY ONE STEP AT A TIME STUDY GUIDE

The *Destined To Be: Walking Into Your God-Given Destiny One Step at a Time Study Guide* by Danyelle Scroggins is designed to help readers dive deeper into their personal journey of discovering and walking in their divine purpose. This faith-filled guide is a companion to the main book, providing practical exercises, reflection questions, and biblical insights that encourage readers to take actionable steps towards fulfilling the destiny God has uniquely crafted for them.

With a focus on overcoming fear, doubt, and procrastination, this study guide leads readers through a process of spiritual growth and self-discovery. It challenges them to break free from distractions, stop comparing themselves to others, and trust God's timing in their lives. Through personal stories, prayer prompts, and scripture-based guidance, Scroggins provides the tools needed to help readers identify their God-given calling and confidently move forward, one step at a time.

Perfect for both individual and group study, the *Destined To Be* study guide is more than just a companion—it's a roadmap for believers ready to stop waiting and start living out their God-ordained purpose.

WELCOME & THANK YOU...

Thank you so much for choosing the *Destined To Be: Walking Into Your God-Given Destiny One Step at a Time Study Guide*! I'm truly honored that you've decided to embark on this transformative journey with me. My hope is that this guide helps you grow closer to God and step confidently into the purpose He has set before you.

How to Use This Study Guide

This study guide is designed to help you go deeper into the principles discussed in the main book, providing practical steps, reflection questions, and personal challenges. Whether you're using it individually or in a group, here are a few simple tips for getting the most out of it:

1. **Follow the sessions at your own pace** – Don't feel pressured to rush through each section. Take your time to fully engage with the content and apply it to your life.

2. Reflect on each topic – After reading the main points and scriptures, take a moment to meditate on how these truths apply to your personal journey. Use the reflection zones to jot down your thoughts, prayers, or any insights God gives you.

3. Pray with Intention – Most sessions end with a prayer. These prayers are meant to serve as a guide for you. Let them be a springboard that leads you into your own heartfelt conversations with God.

4. Journal and Reflect – Use the reflection zones to either Write your thoughts, make notes, or simply take the time to pause and reflect on how God is speaking to you through each lesson.

Let's Walk This Journey Together

As you work through this study guide, my prayer is that you will feel empowered, encouraged, and more in tune with the calling God has placed on your life. Remember, you are not alone on this path—God has already equipped you, and together, we'll take it one step at a time.

Blessings on getting a deeper revelation of who you are in God.

Honor and Glory to our King,

Pastor Danyelle

"For I know the plans that I have for you,' declares the Lord, 'plans for prosperity and not for disaster, to give you a future and a hope."

Jeremiah 29:11

THE BEGINNING (PROLOGUE)

Facing the Truth of Your Calling
The author describes moments when she resisted her true calling, trying to substitute God's plan with her own. Have you ever tried to pursue a path that wasn't truly aligned with your God-given purpose?

WHAT WERE the signs that it wasn't the right path for you?

1.

2.

. . .

3.

4.

5.

Recognizing God's Voice
The author shares how God's voice became louder as she tried to resist her calling. Think back to a time when you felt God speaking to you about your purpose.

How did you recognize His voice, and what was your response?

Are you currently hearing God call you in a specific direction?

The Struggle Between Desire and Obedience
The author was determined to become a firefighter, but ultimately chose obedience to God's calling over her personal desires.

. . .

Is there a dream, goal, or opportunity that you've held onto that might be a distraction from your true calling?

How can you shift from pursuing your desires to pursuing God's will?

Moments of Surrender

The turning point came when the author finally surrendered to God's will and walked away from the firefighter training. Reflect on a time when you had to surrender your plans for something greater.

Reflection:

What was that experience like for you, and how did it impact your relationship with God?

Reflection:

Impact:

. . .

The Power of Support and Resistance

The author had family cheering her on during her firefighter test, but she still had to make the tough decision to quit. How do surrounding people influence your decisions regarding your calling?

Are they pushing you toward God's purpose or encouraging you to stay on a path of personal comfort?

Recognizing Spiritual Cramping

The author experienced physical cramping as a sign that she was out of alignment with her calling. Are there signs in your own life—whether emotional, physical, or spiritual—that suggest you are resisting God's plan?

1.

2.

3.

. . .

WRITE THREE CHANGES you can make to realign with your purpose?

1.

2.

3.

HEARING: **This Is Not the Assignment**

When God told the author that firefighter training wasn't her assignment, she had to come to terms with it. Think about something in your life that may not be your true assignment. What three steps can you take to discern if it's time to walk away or stay committed?

REFLECTION:

1.

2.

. . .

3.

Confronting Your Substitutes

The author tried to substitute firefighting for her true calling. List any "substitutes" you might pursue instead of the calling God has placed on your life.

1.

2.

3.

4.

Write four ways that you can let go of these substitutes and embrace your true purpose?

1.

· · ·

2.

3.

4.

Trusting God's Assignment

The author found peace after accepting her true calling, even though it wasn't the path she initially wanted.

What fears or hesitations do you have about fully trusting God's assignment for your life?

1.

2.

3.

· · ·

How can prayer, reflection, and faith help you overcome these doubts?

Writing Your Own Testimony

The author shares her testimony of surrendering to God's calling. Write your own testimony of a time when you surrendered to God's plan—or if in the process, write about what you hope to gain by surrendering.

Reflection:

Testimony:

Gain:

Discerning Your Calling

Spend time in prayer and reflection, asking God to reveal areas where you may resist your true calling. Journal about what God shows you.

Reflection:

. . .

WRITE THREE WAYS that you can commit to making changes, even if they seem difficult.

1.

2.

3.

AFFIRMING **Your Purpose**

Write a daily affirmation that declares your commitment to embracing the purpose God has assigned to you.

Repeat this affirmation each morning to remind yourself of your true calling and to combat distractions or doubts.

Ex: I am the called of God. I have been chosen for the ministry of healing. I am a serving servant.

Write your first three affirmations here:

1.

2.

. . .

3.

SEEKING Guidance

If you're unsure about your calling, seek guidance from a mentor, pastor, or trusted friend who can help you discern God's voice in your life.

Write four insights or advice they gave to you and how you can apply it on your journey.

1.

2.

3.

4.

SHARING YOUR "FIREFIGHTER" Story

In a group or with a study partner, share your own "firefighter" story—a time when you pursued something other than God's plan for your life.

. . .

WHAT LED you to realize it wasn't the right path, and how did you find the courage to change direction?

WHAT:

HOW:

ENCOURAGING SURRENDER

Discuss the importance of surrendering to God's plan with your group.

REFLECTION:

WRITE THREE WAYS that you can encourage one another to resist distractions and substitutes, and stay focused on God's true assignment?

1.

2.

. . .

3.

Prayer Reflection

After completing the workbook questions, take a moment to pray, using the author's prayer as a guide:

Prayer:

Father, I thank You for revealing Your purpose to me. Help me release any substitutes or distractions that pull me away from Your will. Strengthen me to walk boldly in the calling You have placed on my life, and grant me peace as I surrender fully to You. In Jesus' name, Amen.

1
TAGGED BY HEAVEN

Understanding Divine Identity

The chapter discusses how each person is "tagged by heaven" with a unique purpose and identity. How does this idea resonate with your view of your life's purpose?

1.

2.

3.

. . .

4.

5.

REFLECT ON A TIME when you felt especially connected to a deeper purpose. What factors helped you feel this connection?

1.

2.

3.

Embracing Your Heavenly Tag

The author explains that our heavenly tag, given by God, identifies and sanctifies us. What are some qualities or strengths you believe are part of your "heavenly tag"?

1.

. . .

2.

3.

4.

5.

Are there any life circumstances or challenges that you feel have caused you to drift away from this tag? Describe them and consider how reconnecting with your tag might impact your perspective.

1.

2.

3.

4.

. . .

The Role of Purpose in Overcoming Challenges

The opening illustrates how, despite life's distractions and difficulties, our divine assignment remains constant. Think about a specific challenge you've faced. How might viewing it through the lens of your divine purpose change your approach?

1.

2.

3.

Consider Jeremiah 1:5, which suggests God has known and ordained us even before birth. How does this verse affect your confidence in facing future obstacles?

1.

2.

3.

. . .

Staying Connected to God's Plan

The author emphasizes the importance of staying close to God to keep our "string" untangled. What practices (e.g., prayer, meditation, community) could help you strengthen your connection to God and your purpose?

1.

2.

3.

List three goals or steps you can take in the next month to align more closely with what you believe is your divine purpose.

1.

2.

. . .

3.

IDENTITY BEYOND EARTHLY Labels

Earthly labels (like name tags in the hospital) give us identity, but the author describes a more profound identity marked by heaven. How would you describe the difference between earthly labels (roles, titles, or social identity) and your heavenly tag?

ROLES / Titles / S. Identity

1.

2.

3.

4.

5.

. . .

WHAT PERSONAL LABELS have people assigned to you that you feel don't align with who you are at a deeper level?

1.

2.

3.

REFLECTION ON LIFE'S **Timing and Weight**

The author discusses how a baby's weight, timing, and circumstances all contribute to a larger story. What aspects of your life (your birth circumstances, family background, or pivotal events) seem to align with a greater story or purpose?

A.

B.

C.

. . .

D.

E.

IN WHAT WAYS COULD THE "WEIGHT" of these experiences be part of your journey or assignment?

1.

2.

3.

Closing **Prayer**

Father, I thank You for Your never severing connection to me. Help me to overcome moments when I forget that You will never leave or forsake me, or moments when I fail to recognize that when You are for me, You are more than the world against me. Thank You for the small taps of confirmation being sent to me from those in my circle, things I see, and Your spirit within me. In Jesus's name I pray. Amen.

2
CHOSEN & ASSIGNED

Reflecting on Divine Purpose
The chapter describes how each of us is created with a unique purpose, likened to a "blueprint" crafted by God.

A. What do you believe could be a part of your personal blueprint?

1.

2.

. . .

3.

4.

B. Are there specific qualities or passions within you that feel intentional and purposeful?

1.

2.

3.

Understanding Your Seed

The author compares our potential to a seed, containing everything we're meant to become.

A. What is something within you—a skill, passion, or idea—that feels like a "seed" of purpose?

. . .

1.

2.

3.

4.

5.

B. Describe how nurturing this seed might help you grow closer to fulfilling your assignment.

1.

2.

3.

. . .

STRETCHING BEYOND CURRENT Capacity

Just as the author's grandchild instinctively reached for "five," even beyond her understanding, our spirits can reach beyond what feels achievable.

A. HAVE you ever felt a pull toward something that seems bigger than your current capacity?

B. DESCRIBE this pull and what it means to you.

OVERCOMING CHALLENGES and Growth

The chapter suggests that life challenges often stretch us to our full potential. Reflect on a recent challenge that felt overwhelming.

HOW MIGHT this challenge be a part of your growth towards fulfilling your divine assignment?

1.

2.

. . .

3.

Identifying Your Unique Mission

According to the author, there's a need in the world only you can fulfill. Consider a specific area in your life—whether at work, home, or within your community—where you feel you could make a unique impact.

What steps can you take to further explore or embrace this mission?

1.

2.

3.

Growing Closer to God for Clarity

The author notes that purpose becomes clearer as we grow closer to God. What practices (prayer, meditation, or reflection) could you adopt to deepen this connection and gain more insight into your assignment?

. . .

1.

2.

3.

4.

Recognizing **Your Potential in Adversity**

Sometimes, the tasks or challenges we face feel too big for us. Think of a time when you encountered a situation that seemed beyond your reach, but you pushed through it.

What did you learn about your capacity to grow and adapt, and how might this experience guide you in future challenges?

1

2.

. . .

3.

Crafting a Growth Plan

Based on what you've learned from this chapter, create a simple action plan to nurture your potential. Identify one specific "seed" you want to focus on, along with three steps you can take this month to nurture and grow it.

Seed...

A.

B.

C.

Embracing Your Chosen Identity

The chapter reminds us that our purpose is as unique as our fingerprints.

A. Write one or two statements that affirm your identity and purpose.

1.

2.

B. Write three ways that you can remind yourself daily of these truths, especially when faced with self-doubt?

1.

2.

3.

Processing Past Pain and Prophecy

The author describes hearing painful words from a trusted pastor, but later recognizing them as an unintentional prophecy.

A. Reflect on a challenging situation where someone's words or actions hurt you.

. . .

Looking back, do you see any growth or purpose that may have come from that experience?

YES / NO

If YES, write three things that came from the experience.

1.

2.

3.

Facing Rejection in Pursuit of Purpose

In this chapter, the author is reminded that rejection can sometimes be God's redirection. Think of a time you faced rejection or were removed from a situation that felt right.

In what ways did that experience lead to growth, new opportunities, or a deeper understanding of your purpose?

Growth

. . .

1.

2.

3.

New Opportunities

1.

2.

3.

Deeper Understanding

1.

2.

. . .

3.

Struggle with Calling

The author resisted her calling due to fear and hesitation. Describe an area of your life where you feel pulled toward something significant but have hesitated to pursue it.

A.

B.

What fears or uncertainties are holding you back?

1.

2.

3.

. . .

STEPPING AWAY from Comfort

Following God's direction sometimes means leaving behind comfort, as the author did. Reflect on a situation where you felt called to step out of your comfort zone.

REFLECTION:

WHAT STEPS DID YOU TAKE, or could you take, to trust that God's purpose is greater than your fear?

1.

2.

3.

UNDERSTANDING the Purpose of Struggle

The author explains that struggles and obstacles often prepare us for our purpose.

Reflect on a difficult season you've gone through.

. . .

WHAT STRENGTHS, insights, or skills did you develop through that struggle that now help you in your current life or calling?

1.

2.

3.

PERMISSION TO PURSUE Calling

The author describes receiving "permission" from a pastor to walk in her calling, though she later realized God had already given it.

CONSIDER SOMETHING you feel called to do.

WHO OR WHAT are you waiting for to "give you permission," and how could you begin pursuing this calling now?

1.

. . .

2.

3.

DIVINE PROTECTION in Redirection

When the author's pastor asked her to leave, she later recognized this as God's protection from future limitations. Can you think of a time when something you wanted didn't work out, only to later realize it was for your benefit?

How DID that change your perspective on waiting and trusting God's timing?

LEARNING to Listen

The author speaks about learning to follow God's direction despite her own fears and desires. Identify three specific practices or habits (like prayer, journaling, seeking counsel) that could help you tune into God's guidance, especially when facing difficult decisions.

1.

. . .

2

3.

BLUEPRINT REFLECTION

The author compares the Bible to a "blueprint for better decisions."

Reflect on a specific verse, parable, or teaching that has guided you through a challenging time.

VERSE:

PARABLE:

TEACHING:

HOW MIGHT you rely on this "blueprint" more regularly in future decisions?

RELEASING the Past to Move Forward

The chapter emphasizes letting go of past hurts and delays to fully step into purpose.

List three things—thoughts, habits, or relationships—that you feel may be holding you back.

1.

2.

3.

WHAT STEPS CAN you take this week to release them and make room for growth?

1.

2.

3.

. . .

WHAT ARE your thoughts so far?

CLOSING Prayer

Father, I thank You for Your assignment and for finding me good enough to be used. Help me to overcome the blocks and chains that try to prevent me from Your will. Strengthen me for the assignment and tasks set before me. I have been chosen for a kingdom assignment, and assigned to all good works. In Jesus's name, Amen.

3

HERE'S THE BLUEPRINT

Reflecting on Divine Design
The author compares our lives to the stars and clouds, intricately designed and intentionally placed. Reflect on when you felt connected to a bigger purpose.

THE MOMENT:

WRITE THREE THINGS that the idea of a "blueprint" for your life means to you personally?

1.

. . .

2.

3.

Known Before Birth

Jeremiah 1:5 tells us God knew us before we were born.

Write Jeremiah 1:5:

How does knowing you were "known before you were born" **affect** the way you view your identity or life's purpose?

Reflections:

A.

B.

C.

. . .

DESCRIBE THREE WAYS this knowledge impacts your confidence or direction in life.

1.

2.

3.

SEEING Yourself as God's Masterpiece

Ephesians 2:10 says we are God's "handiwork," created for good works.

WRITE EPHESIANS 2:10

REFLECT on what you see as unique strengths, gifts, or qualities within yourself that might be part of this "masterpiece."

REFLECTION:

. . .

WRITE THREE WAYS that these traits help you live out your purpose.

1.

2.

3.

Understanding Life's Challenges

Romans 8:28 reassures us that everything in life, even hard experiences, works together for God's purpose.

WRITE ROMANS 8:28

THINK of a challenging season you have been through.

CHALLENGING SEASON 1:

CHALLENGING SEASON 2:

. . .

How might that experience be preparing or equipping you for something greater?

A.

B.

C.

D.

Walking in Your Good Works

The "good works" mentioned in Ephesians 2:10 are unique to each of us. What do you feel are the "good works" God has prepared for you to fulfill?

1.

2.

. . .

3.

LIST one or two specific actions you can take this month to live out these good works.

1.

2.

UNDERSTANDING YOUR UNIQUE **Calling**

Isaiah 49:1 states that God calls us by name from our mother's womb.

WRITE ISAIAH 49:1

HOW DOES this personal calling make you feel about your purpose?

. . .

WHAT WOULD CHANGE in your life if you lived each day with the awareness that God has called you by name?

LEARNING to Discern Your Path

The author writes about the importance of discernment in following God's plan. Reflect on how you currently make decisions about your direction.

REFLECTION:

WHAT PRACTICES COULD HELP you seek God's guidance more regularly (e.g., prayer, Bible study, mentorship)?

1.

2.

3.

4.

. . .

5.

6.

7.

Aligning with the Blueprint

The chapter encourages us to align with God's blueprint for abundant living. Think of an area in your life that feels misaligned with what you believe is God's purpose.

THE AREA:

WHAT CHANGES CAN you make to realign with the blueprint God has for you?

CHANGE 1.

CHANGE 2.

. . .

CHANGE 3.

TRUSTING the Process

Getting closer to God reveals more of the blueprint, as emphasized by the author.

LIST THREE WAYS you can seek a closer relationship with God to better understand your purpose (e.g., daily reflection, connecting with a faith community, service).

1.

2.

3.

CHOOSING to Embrace the Blueprint

The chapter concludes by asking whether you're ready to step into your blueprint or live without purpose.

. . .

DESCRIBE ONE STEP you can take this week to embrace God's plan for your life more fully, and how you hope this will influence your journey forward.

THE STEP:

THE INFLUENCE:

CLOSING **Prayer**

Father, I thank You for Your love and devotion toward me. Open my eyes that I may see the steps You have prepared before me. Cause an awareness of Your plan to open in my heart and mind, and cause doors to open or close according to Your plans for me. You know the way. You have the assignment, and the knowledge and wisdom I need is already written in Your Word. Lead me to Your truth and I will be careful to harken unto Your voice. In Jesus's name, Amen.

4
THE TRAP OF ALTERNATIVES

Identifying Your "Safe" Choices
The author speaks about choosing safer, more conventional paths that seem easier than following God's plan.

A. REFLECT on a time in your life when you opted for the "safe" choice.

B. WHAT MOTIVATED THIS DECISION?

C. HOW DID it make you feel in the long term?

. . .

The Ripple Effect of Misalignment

Jonah caused a storm by running from his assignment, bringing chaos to innocent people around him. Think of a time when you felt out of alignment with your purpose.

THE TIME:

DID your choices affect others around you? (Explain How)

1. Yes

2. No

How did this realization impact you?

Resisting God's Plan

The author describes the turbulence that follows when we resist God's blueprint for our lives.

Are there areas in your life where you feel resistance or chaos right now?

. . .

How might you link this to avoiding or delaying God's calling?

Short-Term Fulfillment vs. Long-Term Purpose

Reflect on a situation where you chose something that brought short-term satisfaction but left you feeling empty in the long run.

Reflection:

Name three ways that experience is shaping your understanding of what truly fulfills you?

1.

2.

3.

The Consequences of Alternatives

The author shares how pursuing alternatives to God's plan delayed her progress and brought unnecessary pain.

Can you identify areas where you've pursued alternatives rather than God's purpose?

1.

2.

3.

WHAT WERE the consequences of those choices?

DISTRACTIONS THAT SEEM Appealing

Society often encourages us to pursue material success, relationships, or careers that look good on paper but don't align with our divine purpose.

WHAT ARE some distractions in your life that seem appealing but may pull you away from God's plan?

1.

. . .

2.

3.

4.

5.

EXAMINING Your Relationships

The chapter discusses relationships that seem logical but distract from our true assignment. Think about your current relationships.

ARE there any that feel more like a source of turbulence than support?

HOW MIGHT these relationships be affecting your ability to follow God's blueprint?

REALIGNING with God's Plan

The author urges readers to reflect on where they've chosen

the "safer path" rather than on God's calling. Take a moment to examine your current life choices—career, relationships, or goals.

EXAMINATION:

IN WHAT AREAS do you feel out of alignment with God's plan?

WHAT STEPS CAN you take to realign?

1.

2.

3.

4.

5.

. . .

6.

7.

Recognizing the Cost of "Hits"

The author warns that some "hits" from chasing the wrong things can be devastating and harder to recover from. Consider an experience where pursuing the wrong path caused you emotional, physical, or spiritual harm.

What did you learn, and how will it influence your future decisions?

Trusting God's Blueprint Over Alternatives

The chapter emphasizes that God's plan may not feel safe, but it is the most secure and fulfilling path. Write one area in your life where you feel God is calling you to step out of your comfort zone.

One Area:

. . .

WRITE FOUR WAYS you can begin trusting His blueprint, even if it feels risky.

1.

2.

3.

4.

THE STORY of Jonah Running
   Identifying Your Nineveh
   Jonah ran from Nineveh because the task seemed too difficult. Is there a calling or assignment in your life that you've been avoiding?

NAME SOME THINGS that make this task feel intimidating or overwhelming for you?

1.

. . .

2.

3.

4.

5.

Facing the Consequences of Running

When Jonah fled from God's plan, it caused chaos not only for himself but also for the surrounding sailors. Think about a time when you ran from something God was asking you to do. Did your choice affect the people around you?

How?

Recognizing Your Storms

Jonah's disobedience created a literal storm, threatening his life and the lives of others. Reflect on a situation where your resistance to God's plan caused disruption or turbulence in your life.

. . .

Reflection:

What was the outcome, and how did it impact your sense of peace?

Outcome:

Impact:

Finding Mercy Amid Disobedience

Even though Jonah ran from his assignment, God showed him mercy by sending a great fish to save him.

Have you ever experienced a moment where, despite running from God, you felt His mercy guiding you back?

Describe what that moment was like.

The Ripple Effect of Disobedience

Jonah's choice to run affected everyone on the ship.

How might your disobedience or reluctance to follow God's

calling be affecting those around you—whether in your family, workplace, or community?

1.

2.

3.

The Turning Point in the Fish

Jonah only found peace when he repented in the fish's belly and acknowledged God's authority.

What is your personal "belly of the fish" moment—when you came face-to-face with the consequences of your choices and realized you needed to surrender to God?

1.

2.

3.

. . .

4.

5.

6.

THE POWER of Obedience

After repenting, Jonah received a second chance to fulfill his mission.

A. WHAT ASSIGNMENT or calling in your life have you been avoiding that you now feel ready to confront?

1.

2.

3.

. . .

B. How can you take a step towards obedience today?

1.

2.

3.

Reflecting on Your Storms

The storms that arise from disobedience often disrupt our peace and purpose. Identify an area in your life where you feel resistance or chaos right now.

Area:

What might God be calling you to do that you've been hesitant to obey?

1.

. . .

2.

3.

WRITE one concrete step you can take this week to move toward God's will.

1 STEP:

RELEASING Fear and Doubt

Fear and doubt often lead us to run from God's plans.

List the fears or doubts that are holding you back from fully embracing your calling.

1. Fear or Doubt:

2. Fear or Doubt:

3. Fear or Doubt:

. . .

4. Fear or Doubt:

FOR EACH ONE, write a truth from scripture that can help you counter those fears (e.g., "God did not give us a spirit of fear" – 2 Timothy 1:7).

1.

2.

3.

4.

STEPPING BACK INTO Alignment

The chapter emphasizes God will always provide a way back when we submit to His plan. Think of one area of your life where you need to realign with God's purpose.

AREA:

. . .

WHAT IS one immediate action you can take to walk back toward the path He has set for you?

1 ACTION:

EMBRACING YOUR ASSIGNMENT

Jonah had to face his assignment a second time. Identify an area in your life where you feel God is giving you a second chance to step into your calling. What do you need to do to fully embrace it this time, and how can you ensure you remain obedient going forward?

SHARING YOUR "JONAH" Story

In small groups or with a study partner, share a personal "Jonah" story—an assignment from God that you initially resisted or fled from. How did running affect you and those around you? What ultimately brought you back to God's path?

ENCOURAGING OBEDIENCE in Each Other

Discuss as a group way you can support and hold each other accountable in staying obedient to God's calling.

. . .

How can you encourage one another to avoid running from the assignments God has placed on your lives?

What are your thoughts?

Closing Prayer

Father, I thank You for being all knowing and powerful. You have placed before me a choice to do or not to do. Please lead me to choose the choices that bring You glory. Tear down every alternative in my life and make the way You has chosen shine as bright as the morning sun. In Jesus's name, Amen.

5

DISTRACTIONS THAT PULL

Recognizing Restlessness and Unfulfillment
The author describes restlessness as a sign that you're being pulled away from your purpose. Think of a time when you felt unsettled or unfulfilled in your life—whether at work, in relationships, or in your daily routine.

REFLECTION:

WHAT DO you believe caused this feeling, and how did it affect your pursuit of your God-given purpose?

CAUSE:

. . .

AFFECT:

CHASING Short-Term Wins

Reflect on when you pursued quick success, immediate gratification, or fast solutions over long-term purpose.

REFLECTION:

HOW DID that decision impact you in the long run?

DID IT BRING LASTING FULFILLMENT, or did it leave you feeling empty?

WHAT THREE THINGS did you learn from that experience?

1.

2.

. . .

3.

FACING Unnecessary Obstacles

The author shares constant obstacles can be a sign that you're on the wrong path.

Have you ever encountered a season where it seemed like nothing was going right, no matter how hard you tried?

WHAT MIGHT those obstacles have been telling you about your alignment with God's plan?

1.

2.

3.

SPOTTING Disguised Distractions

Distractions often come disguised as wonderful opportunities or relationships. Identify a "good" opportunity or relationship that, in hindsight, turned out to be a distraction from your true purpose.

. . .

How did it initially appear beneficial, and when did you realize it was pulling you off course?

The Consequences of Validation-Seeking

The author warns against seeking validation from others instead of God. Think of a time when you sought approval from people—whether family, friends, or colleagues—over God's approval.

Reflection:

How did that impact your decisions, and what was the outcome?

Evaluating Busyness as a Distraction

Busyness can often be a distraction from our purpose. Reflect on your current responsibilities and tasks.

A. Are there any activities or commitments that are keeping you busy but not aligned with your purpose?

1.

. . .

2.

3.

B. How can you create more space for what truly matters?

1.

2.

3.

Learning to Say "No"

The author emphasizes the importance of saying "no" to good things in order to say "yes" to the right things. Reflect on a recent opportunity that you had to turn down, or one you're currently considering.

Reflection:

. . .

How did/will you discern if it was the right decision for your purpose?

Staying Rooted in Prayer and God's Word
The author highlights prayer and God's Word as essential for staying aligned with your purpose. How consistent are you in your prayer life and study of the Word?

Identify one specific step you can take to strengthen your connection with God (e.g., setting aside dedicated prayer time, starting a Bible study routine).

1 Step:

Guarding Your Heart and Mind
Proverbs 4:23 tells us to guard our hearts because they determine the course of our lives.

Write Proverbs 4:23:

. . .

Are there any negative influences—such as toxic relationships, media consumption, or unhealthy habits—that are affecting your focus on God's purpose?

1.

2.

3.

How can you guard your heart and mind more effectively?

1.

2.

3.

Surrounding Yourself with Purpose-Driven People

The author encourages surrounding yourself with purpose-driven people. Think about the people you spend the most time with. Are they encouraging you in your purpose, or pulling you away from it?

WRITE FIVE WAYS that you can cultivate more relationships with people who will hold you accountable to your calling?

1.

2.

3.

4.

5.

Keeping the End Goal in Mind

When distractions arise, it's important to keep your focus on the goal. You must remember the "end goal" God has revealed to you about your purpose.

. . .

WRITE ONE AFFIRMATION or scripture that will help you stay focused on that goal during moments of distraction.

SCRIPTURE:

AFFIRMATION:

WRITING Your Own Affirmation

Using the affirmation as inspiration, write another personal affirmation. Focus on declaring your purpose, God's provision, and your commitment to resisting distractions and staying aligned with His plan.

RECOGNIZING Fear and Doubt in Your Life

The author describes how fear and doubt can creep in and weaken your confidence in God's plan.

CAN you identify a time when fear or doubt made you question your calling or abilities?

. . .

How did these emotions affect your decisions or actions?

The Enemy's Tactics

Fear and doubt are tools the enemy uses to keep us stuck. Reflect on a recent situation where fear or doubt tried to hold you back.

Reflection:

How did you respond at that moment?

Did you push through, or did these emotions paralyze you?

Facing Fear While Moving Forward

The author emphasizes you don't have to wait until fear is gone to move forward. Have you ever taken a step of faith, even when fear was present?

Write three ways that experience impacted your faith and confidence in God's ability to guide you?

. . .

1.

2.

3.

Acknowledging Fear, But Not Letting It Stop You

Gideon was afraid, but still obeyed God's call. Think of a current challenge or opportunity that feels overwhelming.

Challenge or Opportunity:

What first step can you take today, despite your fear, to move toward God's calling for your life?

First Step:

Replacing Doubt with Truth

Doubt comes from believing lies about who we are and what God has promised. List some lies that doubt has tried to tell you.

. . .

1.

2.

3.

Write a scripture or truth from God's Word that counters it (e.g., "I am not enough" vs. "I am fearfully and wonderfully made" – Psalm 139:14).

1.

2.

3.

Focusing on God's Ability, Not Yours

The author reminds us to focus on God's ability rather than our own. Reflect on an area in your life where you feel inadequate.

. . .

REFLECTION:

How can shifting your focus to God's sufficiency help you overcome doubt and move forward?

Taking One Step at a Time

The author shares how breaking down larger tasks into smaller steps helps overcome fear.

What is one specific step you can take today toward fulfilling your purpose, even if the entire journey feels overwhelming?

Setting Up Stones of Remembrance

In Joshua 4, the Israelites set up memorial stones to remember God's faithfulness. Think back to times in your life when God came through for you in difficult situations.

REFLECTION:

Write 2-3 "stones of remembrance" to remind you of God's faithfulness in the past, and place them where you can see them when doubt arises.

. . .

1.

2.

3.

Surrounding Yourself with Encouragers

The people you spend time with can either strengthen or weaken your faith. Identify the people in your life who encourage you and speak life to you.

How can you spend more time with these individuals?

Are there any relationships that you need to distance yourself from because they foster doubt?

Using God's Word as a Weapon

When the devil tempted Jesus, He responded with scripture. Write 3-5 key scriptures that address your fears and doubts.

. . .

1.

2.

3.

4.

5.

MEMORIZE THESE VERSES and use them as "word bullets" when fear and doubt try to speak into your life.

CONFRONTING Your Fears

Journal about the specific fears and doubts you are currently facing.

I AM FACING DOUBT ABOUT:

I FEAR:

. . .

BE honest with yourself about how they are affecting your ability to walk in your purpose.

WRITE ONE ACTION you can take this week to confront these fears and move forward in faith.

1 ACTION:

AFFIRMING God's Promises
Use the following affirmation or create your own to declare victory over fear and doubt:
"I trust in God's plan for my life. Fear and doubt have no power over me. I am chosen, called, and equipped by God. I will move forward in faith, knowing that His strength is greater than my weakness. God is faithful, and His promises for me are true. Fear will not paralyze me—I will walk boldly in my purpose."

CREATE YOUR OWN:

CELEBRATING Progress
Overcoming fear and doubt is a process, and each step

forward is worth celebrating. Write your victories—moments when you pushed past fear or doubt—and take time to thank God for the progress you've made.

How can you celebrate these moments with others who are supporting you?

Closing **Prayer**

Father, I thank You for Your truth and Your promises. Help me overcome fear and doubt by trusting in Your Word and Your faithfulness. Strengthen me to move forward in faith, even when I feel afraid or uncertain. Surround me with people who will encourage me and remind me daily of the perfection of Your power in my weakness. In Jesus's name, Amen.

6
THE STORY OF MOSES: RELUCTANCE

Feeling Unqualified
Like Moses, many of us feel unqualified when God calls us to something bigger than ourselves.

REFLECT ON A TIME when you felt unworthy or unqualified for a task or purpose God placed in your life.

REFLECTION:

HOW DID YOU RESPOND, and what were your biggest fears or doubts?

. . .

Recognizing God's Call

Moses was living a quiet life when God called him at the burning bush. How do you think God is calling you in this season of your life?

Are there moments where you feel a "burning bush" experience but hesitate to respond?

Why?

Who Am I?

Moses' first response to God's call was, "Who am I?" (Exodus 3:11).

Write Exodus 3:11:

Reflect on the times when you've questioned your identity or ability in the face of a challenge.

Reflection:

. . .

How can you shift your focus from your limitations to God's presence and power in your life?

Overcoming Rejection and Doubt

Moses feared people wouldn't believe him or recognize his calling (Exodus 4:1).

Write Exodus 4:1:

Have you ever feared rejection or doubt from others regarding your calling?

How did you handle it, and what signs of God's presence can you now see in your life that confirm your purpose?

"I'm Not Good Enough"

Moses believed he wasn't eloquent enough to lead (Exodus 4:10).

Write Exodus 4:10

. . .

Is there a specific skill, talent, or trait you feel you lack that is holding you back from fully stepping into your calling?

How does God's assurance in Exodus 4:11-12—"I will help you speak and will teach you what to say"—encourage you to move forward?

Pleading for an Escape

Despite God's reassurances, Moses still pleaded with God to send someone else (Exodus 4:13). Think of a time when you asked God to release you from a challenging assignment.

Reflection:

A. What was the outcome?

B. How can you trust God knows exactly why He chose you for that task?

God's Response to Excuses

Moses presented four excuses: "Who am I?" "What if they don't believe me?" "I'm not good enough," and "Please send someone else." Write any excuses or reasons you've used to avoid stepping into God's calling.

1.

2.

3.

4.

5.

For each excuse, write how God's response to Moses might apply to your situation.

1.

2.

. . .

3.

4.

5.

Seeing Beyond Limitations

God sees beyond our limitations and equips those He calls. What specific weaknesses or limitations are you currently focusing on?

How can you shift your focus to God's ability to equip you in those areas?

Trusting God's Provision

God provided Moses with signs, a staff, and Aaron to help him. Think about a time when God provided exactly what you needed, even if it wasn't in the way you expected.

Reflection:

. . .

WRITE what you learned from that experience and how it can help you trust His provision in your current situation.

1.

2.

3.

TAKING the First Step

Moses didn't feel ready, but God asked him to trust and obey. What is the first step of obedience you can take today toward the assignment God has placed in your life?

COMMIT TO TAKING THAT STEP, trusting that God will guide you through the next one.

DISCUSSING Reluctance and Faith

In a group or with a partner, discuss a time when you felt reluctant to follow God's calling.

. . .

How did your reluctance manifest—was it through fear, doubt, or feeling unqualified?

How did God reassure you, and what resulted from stepping into faith?

Trusting God's Call on Your Life

Moses eventually led Israel to freedom, even though he doubted his ability.

What significant task has God placed before you that feels beyond your ability?

Write one action you can take this week to trust that God has already equipped you for this assignment, even if it feels overwhelming.

Finding Your "Aaron"

Just as God provided Aaron to support Moses, who is someone in your life that can help you fulfill your calling?

. . .

How can you reach out to this person for encouragement, mentorship, or practical support in moving forward?

Affirming God's Qualification

Declare the following affirmation (or write your own) daily:

I am called by God, not based on my qualifications, but on His purpose. I trust God sees beyond my weaknesses and will equip me with everything I need. Fear and doubt will not stop me from fulfilling my calling. I confidently believe that God's strength becomes perfect in my weakness, and I will progress with faith.

Closing Prayer

Father, I thank You for the calling You have placed in my life. Help me trust that, just as You equipped Moses, You will equip me for the purpose You have given me. Remove the fear and doubt that tries to hold me back, and fill me with the courage to step forward in faith. I surrender my weaknesses to You, knowing that Your power is greater than my limitations. In Jesus' name, Amen.

7

TRUSTING GOD'S TIMING

Embracing God's Timing
The author emphasizes that "God's timing is perfect," but waiting often feels like a challenge. Think about a time when you struggled with waiting for God's timing.

REFLECTION:

HOW DID it affect your relationship with Him and others?

TRUSTING During Delays
God's delays are not denials, but they can feel frustrating.

Reflect on a situation in your life where you felt like God was delaying an answer.

Reflection:

How did you handle that delay?

What do you think God was trying to teach or prepare you for during that time?

The Danger of Rushing

Abraham and Sarah rushed ahead of God's plan and faced unintended consequences. Have you ever tried to take matters into your own hands because you were tired of waiting?

What was the result?

How did it impact your faith journey?

Learning from Biblical Examples

The stories of Joseph, David, and Hannah are powerful

examples of waiting on God's timing. Which of these stories resonates with you the most and why?

How does this example encourage you to stay patient in your current season of waiting?

Handling Impatience

The author shares personal struggles with waiting and watching others succeed while feeling stuck. Reflect on moments when impatience has caused you to feel frustrated or jealous of others' success.

Reflection:

How can you refocus your mind on trusting God rather than comparing yourself to others?

Maintaining Faith **During Waiting**

Hebrews 11:1 says, "faith is the substance of things hoped for, the evidence of things not seen."

How does this verse encourage you in moments when you can't see God's plan?

. . .

WHAT FOUR PRACTICAL steps can you take to strengthen your faith while you wait?

1.

2.

3.

4.

Staying Productive While Waiting

The author suggests ways to stay spiritually aligned while waiting for God's timing. What activities—such as staying in the Word, serving others, or reflecting on past faithfulness—can you incorporate into your daily routine to stay productive and faithful during the waiting season?

Praying for Patience and Discernment

Patience and discernment are key in waiting for God's timing. Take a moment to reflect on how patient you've been in your current season of waiting.

. . .

REFLECTION:

WRITE a four-part prayer asking God for increased patience and discernment to recognize His will as you continue to wait.

PART 1.

PART 2.

PART 3.

PART 4.

SERVING While You Wait

Serving during the waiting season can be a way to keep your focus on God and away from worry. What opportunities for service can you engage in while you wait?

HOW CAN SERVING others help you trust God's timing?

. . .

REFLECTING on God's Past Faithfulness

Reflecting on experiences when God came through can strengthen your faith. Write two or three moments when God's timing was perfect in your life, even if it felt delayed.

1.

2.

3.

How can these examples give you peace in your current situation?

SURROUNDING Yourself with Encouragement

Who in your life helps encourage you to trust in God's timing?

IDENTIFY A PERSON or community that supports you and encourages your faith.

. . .

How can you lean on them for spiritual and emotional support during this season of waiting?

Sharing Your Waiting Story

In a group or with a partner, share a time when you struggled with waiting for God's timing.

Sharing:

What did you learn from that experience, and how did it affect your faith?

How can others in the group support you in your current season of waiting?

Identifying Areas of Impatience

Write specific areas in your life where you're feeling impatient about God's timing.

How can you surrender these concerns to God in prayer?

. . .

WHAT IS one practical step you can take this week to release control and trust His timing?

STAYING FOCUSED on God's Promises

The author mentions the importance of keeping faith in God's promises. Find (2) a scripture or promise that speaks to you about waiting for God.

SCRIPTURE OR PROMISE:

SCRIPTURE OR PROMISE:

WRITE it down and place it somewhere visible as a reminder to trust Him daily.

WHERE WILL you write or place it?

PLANNING YOUR NEXT Faith Step

Waiting doesn't mean being inactive.

What is the next faith-filled step you can take while waiting for God's timing?

WHETHER IT'S SERVING, learning, or stepping out in faith, write one action you can commit to this week that aligns with God's purpose for your life.

1 ACTION:

AFFIRMING Trust in God's Timing

Declare the following affirmation (or write your own) to speak daily:

I trust in God's perfect timing. Even when the answers seem delayed, I know His plan is greater than my own. I will remain patient, faithful, and obedient, knowing that God is preparing me for something far beyond what I can see. I will not rush or delay His purpose. In His timing, everything will come to pass.

CLOSING PRAYER:

Father, I trust in Your perfect timing. Help me remain patient and faithful as I wait for Your plan to unfold. I surrender my impatience and desire for control, knowing that You see the full picture and that Your timing is always for my good. Strengthen my faith, guide my steps, and remind me daily of Your faithfulness. I pray in the name of Jesus. Amen.

8
COMPARISON: THE ENEMY OF PURPOSE

The Trap of Comparison
Reflect on a time when you compared your life to someone else's—whether on social media, at work, or even in your church.

REFLECTION:

WHAT SPECIFIC AREAS of your life did you feel insecure about?

HOW DID this comparison affect your mood, mindset, or faith?

. . .

LOSING Sight of Your Journey

The author mentions that comparison distracts us from the unique path God has set before us.

ARE there any moments in your life where you feel comparison has caused you to lose sight of your own goals or purpose?

How CAN you refocus on the path God has for you?

MEASURING PROGRESS

Think about the ways you've measured your progress in life. Are you using external standards (like other people's accomplishments) or internal standards (based on your personal growth and God's plan)?

How CAN you measure your life by God's standards instead of the world's?

THE DANGERS of Social Media

Social media can often create a filtered reality, making it easy to compare our behind-the-scenes to others' highlight reels.

. . .

How often do you feel inadequate after scrolling through social media?

What boundaries or breaks could you set to help avoid this trap?

Understanding God's Timing

The author discusses trusting God's timing and the struggle of feeling left behind when others seem to advance. Reflect on a season where you felt like others were moving ahead while you were waiting.

Reflection:

How did you cope with these feelings, and how can you trust that God's timing is perfect?

Saul vs. David: The Comparison Trap

Saul's jealousy of David led him down a path of insecurity and distraction.

Have you ever envied someone else's success?

. . .

HOW CAN you shift from feelings of jealousy to celebrating others' victories, knowing that their success doesn't diminish your own?

YOUR UNIQUE JOURNEY

"Your journey might resemble, but it is not anyone else's," declares the author.

Reflect on how your journey has been different from those around you.

REFLECTION:

HOW CAN you celebrate the unique aspects of your path?

WRITE THREE THINGS that make your journey special.

1.

2.

. . .

3.

Rooting Yourself in Your Identity in Christ

Comparison often stems from forgetting our identity in Christ. Take a moment to write out a list of affirmations that remind you of who you are in Christ (e.g., "I am fearfully and wonderfully made," "I am chosen and loved by God," etc.).

1.

2.

3.

4.

5.

6.

. . .

How can you incorporate these truths into your daily routine to stay grounded in God's perspective of you?

Practicing Gratitude

The author highlights gratitude as a powerful antidote to comparison. Write five things you are grateful for in this season of your life.

1.

2.

3.

4.

5.

How can practicing gratitude help you shift your focus away from what you don't have and on the blessings God has already provided?

. . .

SETTING Social Media Boundaries

If social media triggers comparison for you, consider setting boundaries. What are some practical steps you can take to protect your mental health while engaging on these platforms (e.g., limiting screen time, unfollowing certain accounts, fasting from social media for a week)?

1.

2.

3.

4.

5.

6.

. . .

Celebrating Others' **Success**

Reflect on someone whose success has stirred up comparison or jealousy in your heart.

Reflection:

Instead of feeling envious, write three things you admire about their journey and pray for their continued success.

1.

2.

3.

How can celebrating others' victories change your perspective on your own journey?

Discussing **Comparison**

In a group or with a partner, share a time when comparison stole your joy or distracted you from your purpose.

. . .

How did you overcome those feelings?

What strategies can you share with others to help them avoid the trap of comparison?

1.

2.

3.

Supporting Each Other's Journey

How can you, as a group, support one another in staying focused on your individual paths without falling into comparison?

Discuss ways to celebrate each other's progress while keeping the focus on your own God-given purpose.

. . .

1.

2.

3.

4.

5.

IDENTIFYING Comparison Triggers

Write the specific things that trigger comparison in your life (e.g., certain social media accounts, conversations with specific people, etc.).

1.

2.

3.

. . .

4.

5.

How can you intentionally avoid or limit exposure to these triggers?

1.

2.

3.

Affirming Your Journey

Reflect on the statement, "Your purpose is too important to be derailed by someone else's progress."

Write an affirmation that you can say each day to remind yourself that your path is unique and God's plan for your life is unfolding in His perfect timing.

*

*

*

Building a Gratitude Habit

Every day for the next week, write three things you are grateful for in your personal journey.

1.

2.

3.

. . .

REFLECT on how focusing on gratitude changes your mindset and helps you combat the temptation to compare yourself to others.

REFLECTION:

AFFIRMING Your Purpose

I am uniquely made for a purpose that only I can fulfill. My journey cannot be compared to others, but I will trust in God's perfect timing for my life. I celebrate others' successes without feeling threatened, and I remain grateful for the blessings God has given me. My path is unfolding as it should, and I trust that God's plan for me is good.

Closing Prayer:

Father, I thank You for the unique purpose You've placed in my life. Help me stop comparing myself to others and to trust in the path You have for me. Remove any jealousy, insecurity, or doubt from my heart, and fill me with contentment and gratitude. Remind me daily of my identity in You and strengthen my faith as I wait on Your perfect timing. In Jesus' name, Amen.

PROCRASTINATION A SILENT THIEF

Identifying Procrastination
Reflect on a time when procrastination held you back from completing a task or stepping into God's calling for your life.

REFLECTION:

WHAT WAS the main reason for your delay (fear, doubt, lack of confidence, etc.)?

1.

. . .

2.

3.

4.

The Cost of Procrastination

Think about a specific situation in your life where procrastination impacted your progress, either spiritually, personally, or professional.

What opportunities did you miss?

How did this delay affect your growth or purpose?

Recognizing the Root Cause

The author mentions that procrastination often stems from fear. What fear (fear of failure, fear of success, fear of inadequacy) do you struggle with the most?

How has this fear kept you from stepping forward in faith?

. . .

I'll Do It Tomorrow Mentality

Have you ever caught yourself saying, "I'll do it tomorrow"?

WHAT ARE some dangers of this mentality?

1.

2.

3.

4.

How can you combat this mindset with a sense of urgency to accomplish what God has set before you today?

1.

. . .

2.

3.

4.

THE PARABLE of the Talents

In Matthew 25:14-30, the third servant buried his talent out of fear.

READ MATTHEW 25:14-30

HOW DOES this story resonate with your own experiences of delaying action?

WHAT "TALENTS" has God given you that you may be "burying" out of hesitation or fear?

GOD'S TIMING vs. Procrastination

The author mentions that procrastination delays God's plans

for our lives. Reflect on a time when you procrastinated and felt like you missed out on an opportunity.

REFLECTION:

How can you trust God's timing while also avoiding procrastination?

Setting Small, **Faith-Based Goals**

Think of a task or calling that you've been procrastinating on. Break it down into smaller, faith-based goals you can achieve one step at a time.

Write the first step you can take this week to move forward.

Accountability

Identify a trusted person (friend, mentor, pastor) who can help hold you accountable.

Who:

. . .

How will you communicate your goals to them?

What specific steps will you ask them to check in on to ensure that you stay on track?

Taking Immediate Action

What is one action you can take today—right now—that will move you closer to fulfilling a calling or goal you've been putting off?

Make a commitment to take that action and write it down as a reminder.

Write It:

The Power of Accountability

In a group or with a study partner, share a goal or task you've been procrastinating on.

How can the group hold you accountable in a loving and supportive way?

. . .

DISCUSS WAYS TO provide encouragement and check-ins with one another.

BREAKING the Cycle Together

Discuss the importance of breaking the procrastination cycle. Share practical strategies that have worked for you or others in overcoming procrastination.

WHAT HABITS CAN the group develop to avoid procrastination in the future?

PINPOINTING the Root Cause

Reflect on what causes your procrastination.

REFLECTION:

WRITE the specific fears or obstacles that are holding you back from taking action.

FEAR OR OBSTACLE:

. . .

PRAY FOR GOD'S guidance to help you overcome these barriers.

CREATING A TIMELINE

Set a specific timeline for a goal you've been procrastinating on.

DATE:

DATE:

WRITE the small steps and deadlines that will help you move forward.

HOW WILL you ensure you stay committed to these deadlines?

EMBRACING GOD'S **Timing**

How can you differentiate between waiting on God's timing and procrastinating?

WRITE a prayer asking God for discernment in recognizing His timing and the courage to act when He says "Go."

Affirmation

Declare Your Victory Over Procrastination "I will no longer allow procrastination to steal my purpose. I trust in God's perfect timing and have faith that He will equip me for every step of the journey. Today, I will take action and move forward in obedience, knowing that the plans He has for me are good. I will not delay—today is the day to fulfill my calling."

What are your thoughts?

Closing Prayer:

Father, I ask for Your help in overcoming the spirit of procrastination in my life. Reveal to me the areas where I've been delaying and give me the strength and courage to take action. Help me trust Your timing and move forward in faith, knowing that You have equipped me with every step. Keep me accountable and aligned with Your purpose. In Jesus' name, Amen.

10

DISCERNING YOUR DIVINE ASSIGNMENT

Each of us has a divine purpose—a specific assignment that only we can fulfill.

Discerning that assignment can feel overwhelming. Seeking the pieces that complete the puzzle can be challenging, but God has equipped us with the tools, pieces, picture, and the guidance we need to uncover it. Understanding your unique calling isn't just about figuring out what you want to do in life. No, it's not. It's about discovering the deeper mission God has written in your soul.

The first step in discerning your divine assignment is to recognize that you have one.

What are you called to do?

BUT HOW DO you uncover this calling?

. . .

START BY REFLECTING on the areas in your life where you feel a deep sense of fulfillment and joy.

REFLECTION:

WHAT ARE the skills that come naturally to you?

1.

2.

3.

4.

WHAT CAUSES or opportunities stir up passion in your heart?

1.

. . .

2.

3.

4.

What makes you smile the brightest?

1.

2.

3.

4.

What makes you feel the most fulfilled?

. . .

1.

2.

3.

4.

God often reveals our assignments through these inclinations, using them to guide us toward the work we do. For all four questions, I have not one answer but two: Preaching and Writing.

Take a moment to consider the unique gifts and passions God has placed within you. These are not random pieces of your fabric. God has intentionally woven these things into the fabric of your being for His purpose. The things you're passionate about are clues to your divine assignment. Maybe it's a love of teaching, serving, or encouraging others. Or perhaps you have a talent for creating, leading, or problem-solving. These gifts glorify God and serve others.

Guiding Questions and Self-Reflection

To help you discern your calling, ask yourself these reflective questions:

What activities bring me the most joy and fulfillment?

1.

2.

3.

4.

WHAT SKILLS or talents come naturally to me?

1.

2.

3.

4.

. . .

WHAT DO others often come to me for advice or help with?

1.

2.

3.

4.

WHAT CAUSES or problems in the world stir up passion or frustration within me?

1.

2.

3.

. . .

4.

WHERE HAVE I seen God's hand moving in my life, opening doors or providing opportunities?

1.

2.

3.

4.

WHEN I PRAY about my future, what thoughts or visions does God consistently place on my heart?

1.

. . .

2.

3.

4.

REFLECTING on Your Journey

Before identifying your divine assignment, it's important to reflect on your experiences and where God has brought you so far. Think about the pivotal moments, both joyful and challenging, that have shaped your faith journey.

REFLECTION:

WHAT EXPERIENCES or moments in your life have made you question or seek your purpose?

1.

2.

. . .

3.

HAVE THERE BEEN SPECIFIC JOBS, roles, or paths that you pursued but later realized weren't your true calling?

1.

2.

3.

WHAT LED you to that realization?

1.

2.

3.

. . .

Recognizing Your Calling

Sometimes our calling becomes clear through unexpected situations, just like the moment in jail when you realized you were called to preach. God often speaks to us through life's interruptions.

Have you ever experienced an unexpected situation or encounter where you felt God was leading you in a new direction?

Write about when you felt uncertain or afraid to step into what you felt God was calling you to do.

How did you overcome it?

The Role of the Holy Spirit in Revealing Your Purpose

The Holy Spirit plays a key role in guiding us into all truth, including our divine assignments. He brings clarity, peace, and boldness to follow God's calling.

Reflect on a time when you felt the Holy Spirit guiding you or speaking to you.

Reflection:

. . .

WHAT DID THAT FEEL LIKE, and what did you learn from the experience?

How CAN you better invite the Holy Spirit into your decision-making and discernment process?

SCRIPTURE MEDITATION: John 16:13
"But when He, the Spirit of truth, comes, He will guide you into all the truth."

SPEND A FEW MOMENTS IN PRAYER, asking the Holy Spirit to guide you into the truth of your calling.

WRITE ANY THOUGHTS or feelings that come up during this time.

1.

2.

3.

. . .

4.

Prayer, Meditation, and Journaling

Clarity often comes through spending intentional time in prayer and reflecting on scripture. Writing your thoughts can reveal patterns and passions that align with your calling.

What scriptures do you turn to when you feel unsure about your path?

1.

2.

3.

Reflect on Jeremiah 29:11 and ask God to reveal His plans for you.

Write Jeremiah 29:11:

. . .

JOURNAL about your current feelings of purpose. Whereas it concerns purpose, I feel...

1.

2.

3.

4.

WHAT OPPORTUNITIES HAVE ARISEN RECENTLY that seem to align with your gifts and passions?

1.

2.

3.

Strategies for Clarifying Your Assignment

Practical steps like prayer, journaling, and seeking community can help clarify your assignment.

Clarifying Your Assignment

What recurring themes or passions have emerged as you reflect on your journey?

1.

2.

3.

4.

Write them down again and pray for further clarity as you write.

1.

2.

. . .

3.

4.

THINK ABOUT YOUR UNIQUE GIFTS. How can they be used to serve others and glorify God?

EMBRACING the Process

Discerning your divine assignment is a process, and it often takes time. Trusting God's timing is crucial.

Are you feeling impatient or uncertain about where you're headed?

REFLECT on how you can better trust God's timing in your journey.

REFLECTION:

HOW HAS God shown you patience in your life before?

. . .

USE this reflection to encourage yourself to stay faithful in the waiting.

WALKING in Your Purpose

God has placed a unique calling on your life, and through reflection, prayer, and community, you can step confidently into that purpose. Trust that God will guide you through the Holy Spirit and the people He places in your life to confirm your path.

Final Reflection:

As you look back on your journey and this workbook, what have you learned about your calling?

WRITE your next steps toward walking confidently in your assignment.

WHAT ARE you most excited about as you move forward in your purpose?

11

SURROUNDING YOURSELF WITH THE RIGHT PEOPLE

Reflecting on Your Current Circle

Take some time to assess your relationships. Who are the people currently in your circle, and how are they influencing your spiritual and personal growth?

Activity 1: Relationship Assessment

Make a list of the five people you spend the most time with.

1.

2.

3.

· · ·

4.

5.

ANSWER the following questions for each person:

A. Do they encourage you in your faith or pull you away from it?

PERSON 1.

PERSON 2.

PERSON 3.

PERSON 4.

PERSON 5.

· · ·

B. Do they challenge you to grow spiritually, mentally, and emotionally?

Person 1.

Person 2.

Person 3.

Person 4.

Person 5.

C. Are they pursuing their own God-given purpose?

Person 1.

Person 2.

. . .

Person 3.

Person 4.

Person 5.

D. Do they hold you accountable when you need it?

Person 1.

Person 2.

Person 3.

Person 4.

Person 5.

Reflect on your answers.

. . .

WHICH RELATIONSHIPS ARE HELPING you align with your calling?

1.

2..

3.

WHICH MAY BE HINDERING your growth?

1.

2.

3.

SCRIPTURE REFLECTION—PROVERBS 13:20

"Walk with the wise and become wise, for a companion of fools suffers harm."

ACTIVITY 2: Wisdom Walk

In what ways do you see this verse play out in your life?

1.

2.

3.

WRITE specific examples where walking with wise individuals has positively impacted your life.

1.

2.

3.

. . .

Then, consider times where negative influences caused harm or set you back.

Example 1–Positive **Influence:** Write about a time someone helped you grow in wisdom.

1.

2.

3.

Example 2–Negative **Influence:** Describe a situation where a poor influence led you into harm or away from God's plan.

1.

2.

. . .

3.

IDENTIFYING Your Support System

Surrounding yourself with the right people means finding those who challenge you, pray for you, and hold you accountable.

ACTIVITY 3: Your Faith Network
Answer:
Who in your life has "crazy faith" like Linda Baldwin?

WHO IS knowledgeable about the Word like Superintendent David Gatlin Sr.?

WHO KEEPS you grounded and on track like Diane Kimble Walls Jenkins?

WRITE their names and how they've impacted your journey. If you don't have someone in each category, pray to God to bring these relationships into your life.

PRACTICAL APPLICATION

The Power of Mentorship and Supportive Relationships

Mentors play a crucial role in guiding us through challenges, giving us insight and encouragement.

Activity 4: Reflecting on Your Mentors

Think about mentors you've had. Answer these questions:

How has a mentor helped you stay focused on God's plan?

1.

2.

3.

WHAT ROLE DID vulnerability play in your relationship with this mentor?

HOW DID your mentor help you grow spiritually and personally?

IF YOU DON'T HAVE a mentor yet, Write what you hope to gain from a mentor and how you can take steps to seek one.

. . .

Ruth and Naomi–A Biblical Example of Support

The story of Ruth and Naomi is a powerful illustration of loyalty, support, and divine alignment. Reflecting on this relationship can help us see the importance of walking alongside those who are in pursuit of God's will.

Reflection:

Activity 5: Reflect on Ruth and Naomi

How did Ruth's commitment to Naomi align her with God's plan?

In your own life, who is your "Naomi"—someone who leads and supports you through your faith journey?

Write about how their guidance has impacted you:

1.

2.

. . .

3.

4.

Fostering Healthy, Purpose-Driven Relationships

Healthy relationships require discernment, intentionality, and mutual support. It's also crucial to recognize when it's time to let go of relationships that hinder growth.

Activity 6: Pray for Discernment

Take a moment to pray. Ask God for discernment in your relationships. Ask for clarity on which relationships to nurture and which to distance yourself from.

Activity 7: Letting Go

Is there a relationship in your life that you sense is no longer serving your growth or is pulling you away from God's purpose?

Write about boundaries you can set to protect your spiritual health.

1.

. . .

2.

3.

4.

Action Plan–Building a Godly Community

Building and maintaining healthy relationships requires intention and effort.

Activity 8: Action Steps for Building Community

Write 3 actionable steps you can take to surround yourself with faith-driven individuals.

This could include joining a Bible study group, seeking a mentor, or being more intentional with the people you already know.

1.

2.

· · ·

3.

BUILDING Relationships That Support Your Divine Assignment

What qualities do you look for in relationships that support your spiritual journey?

1.

2.

3.

HOW DO you ensure that the people in your inner circle are in alignment with your divine assignment?

PLAN OF SECURITY:

TAKING Immediate Action

Here are some questions that will lead you into understanding whether you are the type of person who will take action or allow the enemy to fester. Answer truthfully as this will help you gage whether you are ready for the next levels.

How do you "nip the mess in the bud" within your friendships or ministry team?

1.

2.

WHAT STRATEGIES HELP you maintain harmony and unity?

1.

2.

WHY IS it important to make sure the people around you help rather than hinder your ministry or calling?

1.

. . .

2.

WHAT STEPS CAN you take to foster relationships that uplift your spirit and encourage your growth in faith?

1.

2.

IN WHAT WAYS do your closest relationships challenge you to grow spiritually, mentally, or emotionally?

1.

2.

HOW DO they hold you accountable?

. . .

1.

2.

WHAT DOES "BEING ON ONE ACCORD" in friendships or ministry mean to you?

1.

2.

HOW DO you take active measures to maintain this unity in your community?

1.

2.

ARE there any relationships in your life that may no longer serve your growth?

· · ·

1.

2.

WHAT BOUNDARIES COULD you set to protect your spiritual health?

1.

2.

How do you balance being a source of support to others while also ensuring that you surround yourself with people who uplift and challenge you?

1.

2.

· · ·

CLOSING **Prayer**

Father, I thank You for Your the blessed assurance that You will cover and protect me along the journey. Help me be a good neighbor, but also help me discern if my neighbor is for or against You. I understand that those who are against You will be against me. So teach me how to discern my relationships. Teach me how to treat even those who are my enemies. Help me to always remember that I owe no man anything except but to love them. It is this love that will cover their faults, and also cause me to have patience, show kindness, be truthful, uplift, and build others up. In Jesus's name, Amen.

12

WALKING BOLDLY IN YOUR DESTINY

Understanding Boldness in Your Calling

Walking in your God-given purpose requires courage, faith, and determination. Owning your assignment means more than just knowing your purpose—it means stepping into it with confidence.

What fears or uncertainties have you faced as you've tried to walk in your divine assignment?

1.

2.

. . .

3.

How does embracing your calling with boldness differ from simply acknowledging you have a purpose?

Why is it important to have a heart of courage and divine determination when stepping into your destiny?

Breaking Through Fear: Living Fearlessly and Boldly

Fear is one of the most common barriers to walking boldly in your destiny. It can prevent you from taking action and hold you back from fulfilling God's plan for your life. But God hasn't given us a spirit of fear, but of power, love, and a sound mind (2 Timothy 1:7). Overcoming fear is essential to living out your calling.

What types of fear (e.g., fear of failure, fear of rejection) have hindered you from fully embracing your calling?

1.

2.

. . .

3.

4.

How does 2 Timothy 1:7 ("For God has not given us a spirit of fear, but of power, love, and a sound mind") change the way you view fear in your life?

Here are some practical tips for living fearlessly:
   Recognize the Source of Fear.
   Speak God's Promises Over Your Life
   Take Action Despite Fear
   The key to overcoming fear is to take action in faith. Fear is nothing more than an illusion.

Have you ever taken action despite fear?

1.

2.

. . .

3.

WRITE WHAT HAPPENED when you did.

1.

2.

3.

WHAT IS ONE SMALL, faith-filled step you can take today toward fulfilling your calling?

1 STEP:

HOW DOES SPEAKING God's promises over your life help you reject fear and replace it with faith?

PERSONAL EMPOWERMENT and Boldness

Stepping boldly into your destiny is a process of empowerment that comes from trusting God and moving past your fears. As you take steps in faith, your confidence grows and fear diminishes.

Can you recall a time when you took a step of faith and saw doors open as a result?

How did this experience build your confidence in God's plan?

How does trusting in God's strength give you the courage to walk boldly in your purpose?

What is one area of your life where you need to trust God more fully to empower you to fulfill your calling?

Biblical Example: Esther—Courage in the Face of Great Risk

Esther's story is a powerful example of courage in the face of fear. She risked her life to save her people, trusting that God had placed her in her position "for such a time as this."

Reflection:

. . .

How does Esther's courage inspire you to step boldly into your own assignment, even when the risks are great?

What does Esther's story teach you about relying on God's guidance through prayer and fasting when facing fear?

How can you apply Esther's boldness in your own life, especially when the stakes feel high?

Taking Ownership of Your Calling Today

Fully embracing your God-given assignment means taking ownership of it—confessing it, believing in it, and stepping into it with faith.

What three steps can you take to fully accept and embrace the assignment God has placed in your life?

1.

2.

3.

. . .

WRITE THREE WAYS prayer and spending time in God's Word help you gain clarity and confidence in your calling?

1.

2.

3.

SURROUND YOURSELF with Encouragement

Walking boldly into your destiny is not something you can do alone. You need a support system of people who will uplift, encourage, and hold you accountable.

Who in your life encourages and uplifts you in your calling?

1.

2.

3.

. . .

How do they help you stay focused and bold in your purpose?

How can you intentionally build a stronger community of support around you as you walk in your destiny?

What role does accountability play in helping you stay on track with your calling?

Living Fully in Your God-Given Destiny

God has called you to a unique and powerful assignment. Embrace it with boldness, trust in His strength, and surround yourself with people who will encourage you on the journey. Like Esther, step confidently into your destiny, knowing that God has created you for such a time as this, and He is with you every step of the way.

What fears or obstacles are holding you back from walking fully in your God-given destiny? (LIST THEM)

1.

2.

· · ·

3.

WRITE THREE WAYS you can overcome them.

1.

2.

3.

WHAT BOLD STEPS will you take today to walk confidently in your calling?

1.

2.

3.

. . .

How will you continue to seek God's guidance as you pursue your purpose, and what practical actions can you take to ensure you stay in alignment with His will?

Action Plan

What are the top three takeaways you've gained from this study that will help you walk boldly in your destiny?

1.

2.

3.

Write one faith-filled action step you will take this week to live more fully in your calling.

1 Action:

. . .

CLOSING PRAYER:

Father, I thank You for my steps being ordered by You. Your Word is a lamp unto my feet and a light unto my path. Because of this, my way is bright and my eyes shall find only the path You desire for me. Guard my feet, heart, mind, and soul with Your Word, and cause them to stand still when the way is not as clear as it needs to be. Your sheep know Your voice, and we will never follow a stranger's voice or directives. Keep me Father even when I cannot keep myself. In Jesus' name, Amen.

13

THE JOY OF FULFILLING YOUR GOD-GIVEN PURPOSE

This last section of the study guide will help you reflect on and internalize "The Joy of Fulfilling Your God-Given Purpose." Use the questions and activities to deepen your understanding of living in alignment with God's will and the joy it brings.

PART I

THE FULFILLMENT OF WALKING IN GOD'S WILL

Living in your God-given purpose brings a unique sense of fulfillment, joy, and peace that nothing else can provide. This joy surpasses external achievements and rewards.

What does living in alignment with God's will mean to you personally?

Reflection:

Can you recall a time when you felt true peace and joy from walking in your purpose?

. . .

Reflection:

How did that experience differ from other types of success or happiness you've experienced?

Reflection:

Why do you think nothing in this world (money, success, relationships) can compare to the joy of walking in God's assignments?

Reflection:

PART II

OVERCOMING CHALLENGES TO FULFILL YOUR PURPOSE

While walking in your purpose brings joy, the journey isn't always easy. It requires faith, perseverance, and patience, especially when fear, doubt, and uncertainty arise.

What are some challenges you've faced while trying to walk in your God-given purpose?

How does 2 Corinthians 5:7 ("For we walk by faith, not by sight") encourage you to keep going, even when the path seems unclear?

. . .

Why is patience an important aspect of fulfilling your purpose?

Reflect on James 1:3-8.

How can you "let patience have her perfect work" in your life?

PART III

TRUSTING GOD'S TIMING AND PLAN

God's timing is perfect, even when we don't fully understand it. Just as seeds take time to grow, the fruit of your calling will manifest in God's time.

Reflection:

How has trusting in God's timing brought peace during seasons of waiting in your life?

Have there been moments when you doubted God's timing?

. . .

How did you overcome that doubt and continue to trust in His plan?

Galatians 6:9 encourages us not to grow weary in doing good because we will "reap a harvest if we do not give up."

How does this verse inspire you to keep pressing forward?

PART IV

THE RIPPLE EFFECT OF WALKING IN YOUR DESTINY

When you live in your divine purpose, you don't just experience personal joy; your life also becomes a vessel through which God can work to impact others.

Reflection Questions:
How has walking in your purpose influenced the lives of those around you?

Can you think of specific examples where your obedience inspired others to trust in God's plan for their own lives?

. . .

2 Timothy 2:20-21 speaks of being a "vessel of honor, sanctified, and useful to the Master."

How does this scripture motivate you to keep pursuing your God-given assignment?

What legacy of faith do you hope to leave for others through your obedience to God?

PART V
EMBRACING YOUR FULL POTENTIAL

Living in your God-given destiny stretches you beyond what you thought was possible. God empowers you to achieve the extraordinary when you are walking in His strength.

What gifts or talents has God placed in you that come alive when you walk in your purpose?

How has God stretched you to go beyond your comfort zone?

What extraordinary things have you achieved by trusting in His strength rather than your own?

. . .

What remaining doubts or fears do you need to let go of in order to fully embrace the potential God has placed within you?

PART VI

THE ROLE OF FAITH, PATIENCE, AND PERSEVERANCE

Faith, patience, and perseverance are key to fulfilling your purpose. They help you stay the course when challenges arise and the journey gets tough.

How does faith help you keep your eyes on God's promises, especially when you don't have all the answers?

What role does perseverance play in helping you maintain your purpose, even in difficult times?

. . .

Reflect on Galatians 6:9 and how it encourages you to continue.

How do you practice patience while waiting for God's promises to manifest in your life?

What has God taught you in those waiting seasons?

PART VII

STEPPING BOLDLY INTO YOUR CALLING

Now is the time to step fully into your God-given destiny. Trust that God has equipped you with everything you need to succeed and that your journey, while challenging, will bring immense joy and fulfillment.

How can you step forward with confidence into your divine assignment?

What practical steps can you take today to embrace the purpose God has set before you?

. . .

What fears or hesitations do you need to let go of?

How can you trust God has "got you covered" and that He's guiding your steps?

What does walking boldly in your destiny mean to you, and how will you carry that confidence into the future?

PART VIII

LIVING A LIFE OF JOY AND FULFILLMENT

The joy of fulfilling your God-given purpose is lasting and profound. This joy not only carries you through challenges but also enables you to make an eternal impact in the lives of others.

How has living in alignment with God's will bring you joy that surpasses understanding?

What does the phrase "walking in your God-given destiny" mean for your daily life and decisions?

. . .

How can your obedience to God have a lasting impact on others, potentially leading lost souls to Him?

PART IX

ACTION PLAN

As you reflect on the joy and fulfillment of living out your divine assignment, create an action plan for stepping more fully into your purpose.

Identify one faith-filled action you will take this week to step more boldly into your calling. Whether it's having a conversation, starting a new project, or praying more intentionally, take that step in faith.

Write three ways you can practice patience and perseverance as you wait on God's promises to manifest.

. . .

1.

2.

3.

How will you stay encouraged during the waiting season?

List the people in your life who can provide support, accountability, and encouragement as you walk in your purpose.

How can you build or strengthen these relationships?

What is your biggest takeaway from this study on fulfilling your God-given purpose?

How will you continue to seek God's guidance and joy as you move forward in your destiny?

. . .

What are you most excited about as you embrace the fullness of your calling?

Closing Prayer:

Dear Lord, thank You for the calling You have placed in my life. As I walk boldly in my purpose, I ask for Your strength, patience, and guidance. Fill me with joy as I fulfill the assignment You've ordained for me, and let my life be a vessel through which Your love and power can reach others. Help me trust in Your timing and to persevere through every challenge. In Jesus' name, Amen.

ABOUT THE AUTHOR

Danyelle Scroggins is the Senior Pastor of New Vessels Ministries in Shreveport, Louisiana. She is the author of special books like Put It In Ink, Graced After The Pain, Evonta's Revenge, & Enduring Love. She's the wife of Pastor Reynard Scroggins and the mother of three young adults: Raiyawna, Dobrielle, and Dwight Jr. She's privilege to be the grandmother of Emiya'rai Grace.

Danyelle loves writing inspirational stories set in Louisiana, where she lives preaching, teaching, and enjoying writing by the window. Learn all about her here www.danyellescroggins.com.

Also find her on Facebook, Twitter, and Bookbub.

- facebook.com/authordanyellescroggins
- twitter.com/pastordanyelle
- bookbub.com/profile/danyelle-scroggins
- goodreads.com/danyellescroggins

ALSO BY DANYELLE SCROGGINS

THE NONFICTION BOOKS

NOT UNTIL YOU'RE READY https://amzn.to/3TotBdW

HIS MISTRESS OR GOD'S DAUGHTER https://amzn.to/4dwsIC

PROCESSED FOR PURPOSE https://amzn.to/3T2XdYd

40 DAYS OF HEALING https://amzn.to/4cTALrP

A BLACK GIRL'S CRY https://amzn.to/4dyLqJv

THE SUNDAY SERVICE SERIES

YOU CAN'T SLAY STUCK https://amzn.to/4fVqnCs

YOU CAN'T PRAY SCARED https://amzn.to/3TUss8b

STANDALONES

DESTINY'S DECISION https://amzn.to/3Xdg3hR

A HEART ASSIGNED https://amzn.to/3AEUoq8

MORE THAN GRATEFUL https://amzn.to/4fWNYT5

THE POWER SERIES https://amzn.to/3YXUpiS

SOMETHING DIFFERENT https://amzn.to/3YXBzIx

EVONTA'S REVENGE https://amzn.to/3MgIFjR

MORE THAN EXPECTED https://amzn.to/3yQwNlA

PUT IT IN INK https://amzn.to/3T0x1O0

MORE THAN DIAMONDS https://amzn.to/3yGv42l

NOT TOO FAR https://amzn.to/3AyPtXJ

CURVY GIRL VALENTINES

CURVES OR CUPID https://amzn.to/3X5dXPY

CURVY GIRL HOLIDAY SERIES EBOOKS

HIS FOR CHRISTMAS https://amzn.to/3YYENfa

HOPE FOR CHRISTMAS https://amzn.to/3Xe5OKe

HOME FOR CHRISTMAS https://amzn.to/3T2TFFh

HAPPY FOR CHRISTMAS https://amzn.to/4cC56uH

HELP FOR CHRISTMAS https://amzn.to/3T2RmlB

HEALED FOR CHRISTMAS https://amzn.to/4cBHiHq

HALLELUJAH FOR CHRISTMAS https://amzn.to/471Gjza

HONOR FOR CHRISTMAS https://amzn.to/4cF9itN

KATRINA JACOBS MURDER SUSPENSE SERIES

SECRET SECRET https://amzn.to/4dzEI62

DO NOT TELL https://amzn.to/4cz5oSV

IF YOU DO https://amzn.to/3MhXLpl

YOU'LL GO TO JAIL https://amzn.to/3T54KWr

THIS TIME AROUND SERIES

SWEET LOVE https://amzn.to/4fVeD2S

A HEART ASSIGNED & A HEART ASSURED https://amzn.to/4d9zKfn

www.ingramcontent.com/pod-product-compliance
Lightning Source LLC
LaVergne TN
LVHW012016060526
838201LV00061B/4338